Vanquish Ego!

Applying Sun Tzu's 'Art of War'

With 'A Course in Miracles'

Bette Jean Cundiff

Vanquish Ego

C 2019 Bette Jean Cundiff

All Rights Reserved

Miracle Experiences and You Publishers

www.bettejeancundiff.blogspot.com

**ISBN-13:
978-1500656195**

**ISBN-10:
1500656194**

Vanquish Ego

Lesson 1

Introduction:

Strange Bedfellows

Vanquish Ego

On the one hand, *'A Course in Miracles'* and Sun Tzu's *Art of War* and must be the most unlikely pairing possible. However, war by any other name is still war, a battle for supremacy. And it ain't always a pretty sight! And as any serious student of *'A Course in Miracles'* has noticed the ego hangs on tenaciously and viciously in its attempt to keep us focused on its view of ourselves and the world around us.

Ego is an insane, dysfunctional attempt to survive at all costs, wreaking havoc on our emotional stability. *'A Course in Miracles'* is here to show us another way.

In a formal war the goals are usually the same for both sides and the combatants are all too human. But, in the psychological battle for supremacy, the armies on each side are diametrically opposed in goal as well as method.

Vanquish Ego

The goal of ego is control and camouflaged pain. The goal of *'A Course in Miracles'* is freedom and peace. The battle field is the mind, and our bodies and physical world a reflecting mirror of what rages within.

Fascinatingly, the strategies set forth hundreds of years ago in China by a superior commander named Sun Tzu, can be utilized as metaphor in the twenty first century to help us heal our minds. The sparsely worded military tactics of *'The Art of War'* written in the 6th century B.C. marries easily with the spiritual psychology of *'A Course in Miracles'* written in the late 20th Century.

Strange bedfellows for sure. But, like so many unlikely marriages that stand the test of time, these two just seem to work.

Vanquish Ego

Some thoughts to contemplate...

1. Have you been studying 'A Course in Miracles'? Or have you always wanted to start studying 'A Course in Miracles'? Or are you simply intrigued with the title of this book and know little or nothing about the 'Course'?

2. If you are already a student of 'A Course in Miracles' the following lessons can bring you a fresh view of concepts and reinforcement of your studies.

3. If you are unfamiliar with 'A Course in Miracles' then you will find these lessons a solid overview of the spiritual psychology presented in the 'Course' and create a good foundation should you wish to study it in the future.

Vanquish Ego

Lesson 2
Ego's Ninja Warriors

Vanquish Ego

First, we take a quick peak at what the ego has planned for us. Meet Ego's Ninja Warriors. Let's start with this one quote from the 'A Course in Miracles' that speaks of the ego's efforts and the psychological soldiers it uses.

". . .(The ego's) messengers are trained through terror, and they tremble when their master calls of them to serve him. For (this master) is merciless even to its friends. Its messengers steal guiltily away in hungry search. . .for they are kept cold and starving and made very vicious by their master, who allows them to feast only upon what they return to him. No little shred. . .escapes their hungry eyes. And in their savage search . . .they pounce on any living thing they see, and carry it screaming to their master, to be devoured. . .They

Vanquish Ego

have been taught to seek. . .and to return with gorges filled. . ."

Sounds a little like the zombie apocalypse in the latest B movie. But make no mistake. This is a quote from Chapter 19 of the Text, The Attainment of Peace, from 'A Course in Miracles'. Those messengers are the bitter need to find fault in everyone around us and when found, pounce with anger, usually attacking those we seem to love the most.

Ego's Ninja Warriors lurk within all of us salivating at the opportunity to ravage our peace of mind and thus our lives.

Most important, though, is to remember ego is not something or somebody, or some force of nature or the force of evil. Ego is simply an extremely narrow view of ourselves. And when we choose to see ourselves, the world and our interactions only through this truncated viewpoint

Vanquish Ego

our decisions for survival and wellbeing are naturally distorted, twisted and unhealthy.

See survival through this tight focus and paranoia reigns. Ego logic demands soldiers to keep you safe in its now demented and dark shadow world. Guilt, fear, anger and attack are the weaponry for ego's Ninja Warriors and these warriors are trained from childbirth and their skills honed over years of training.

Whew! That's a little dark, but as we review Sun Tzu's advice, offered in the seventh century A.D. for succeeding in combat, we can make superior use of it today when we marry it to the spiritual psychology of 'A Course in Miracles'.

Vanquish Ego

Some thoughts to contemplate...

1. Take time in meditation to ask for the spiritual armor you will need to combat ego.

2. If you are a student of the 'Course' notice how 'A Course in Miracles' doesn't talk only about lightness and goodness. How do you feel about the darker explanations of ego the Course offers?

3. Take note each time you find yourself judging others, sometimes with 'humor' and other times with overt unkindness. Label each correctly as ego's Ninja's Warriors at work in your mind.

Vanquish Ego

Lesson 3

The Peaceful Samurai

Vanquish Ego

You will need to become a samurai to vanquish ego and its Ninja Warriors. Here are some quotes from 'A Course in Miracles' that set the requirements:

"...anyone who chooses to be one (will be one)...qualifications consist only in this; somewhere, somehow he has made a deliberate choice...once he has done that his road is established, and his direction is sure...The Call is universal...Many hear it but few will answer."

In 'A Course in Miracles' these samurais are called teachers of God. (And the above quotes come from Volume Three, Manual for Teachers. The whole manual is an excellent source for learning your role as a teacher of God, or in this case a Peaceful Samurai.)

Vanquish Ego

Now, back to becoming a samurai, a Peaceful Samurai. You have been called. Have you answered? Well, since you are reading this little mini-course we can safely assume you have. Great, you have enlisted.

Wouldn't it be wonderful if all we needed to do is want something and there it was, plopped down in front of us ready for the taking, or in this case the becoming. After all, we become a 'teacher of God' aka Peaceful Samurai was soon as we choose. Right?

Well, not quite. We will need to desire it, be dedicated to it and be disciplined permanently to its accomplishment.

Oh, and we need to understand exactly what being a samurai, battling ego, is really about. To understand all that you will need to show up at boot camp. A peaceful samurai will have a very unique skill set. You will become the special forces combatant for the healing of your mind.

Vanquish Ego

The battle ground will always be within your own mind. You will be fooled into believing that the nasty neighbor, the blind justice system, the maniacal dictator, or your failing body is the enemy and you must meet this enemy on its own turf. Certainly, over centuries the Art of War has been used by generals, commanders, leaders of state and today Wall Street warriors to tackle the forces lined up against them.

But, wait. This is not the battle ground we will be engaged on. And just like the line from the poem, 'A Road Less Traveled', we will choose differently, 'and that will make all the difference.'

Some thoughts to contemplate...

1. Have you already noticed that you have been called in some way to be of service to others? What was that like?

Vanquish Ego

2. Since you have already make a decision to become a Peaceful Samurai (or you would not be reading this) take some time to contemplate the strength of your commitment to this goal.

3. Take some time to track how often you see enemies around you are and are tempted to enter into battle with words, actions or even with just judgmental thoughts.

Vanquish Ego

Lesson 4

To win, Sun Tzu says:

Keep your friends close,

and your enemy even closer.

Vanquish Ego

Thanks to Hollywood just about everyone has heard this saying from The Art of War at least once and usually can quote the last tricky part – keeping those troublesome enemies closer. Back in the day, Sun Tzu was strategizing bloody battles. Let's see how we can unpack Sun Tzu's sayings and reformulate them for our amorphous thinking processes.

Our battleground will be within the unlimited and cloudlike substance of our thoughts. We can train our bodies to be superior fighting machines with skills and stamina. But now our training must include totally different skills and a stamina that must last through the constant and vigilant attacks of ego.

Remember ego is a persistent opponent. Its greatest strength is its own belief that what it does it does to protect you and help you survive. The myopic, limited view of ego is actually our mind

Vanquish Ego

choosing to see with tunnel vision. We block out the whole and see only the now twisted and distorted right in front of us. This leads directly to a perceived a world of lack, need, greed, attack and pain. Survival is paramount and ego shows us how.

So, why should we keep this unpleasant enemy closer than even our beloved friends? After all, ego is already as close as you can get. Ego pervades and directs our beliefs, perceptions and ultimately our actions.

You keep someone close by understanding them fully and in the understanding comes the answers you will need to win.

Beloved friends are easy to like and easy to love. They are easy to forgive, and we usually find their pesky quirks kind of cute. We love keeping them near. But, all those others? The ones that are annoying, irritating, causing pain and havoc in our lives? They are obnoxiously repulsive and we

Vanquish Ego

either turn our backs on them or beat them to a pulp.

When it come to our own thoughts, we do the same thing. We hold onto the ones that give us pleasure and ignore or battle the ones we find offensive. Denial and battle, however, will not bring an end to the emotional pain we live with daily.

There must be another way. We must do something else. We must choose first to look closely at ego and how it works. We must get very, very close to it indeed and apply something totally radical, something miraculous.

As 'A Course in Miracles' says in Chapter 2, "The escape from darkness involves two stages. . This (first) step usually entails fear. . .This (second) step brings escape from fear. . .When you have become willing to hide nothing. . you will understand peace and joy.

Vanquish Ego

Some thoughts to contemplate...

1. Take some time to survey your willingness to handle your issues first with your mind, rather than with immediate action. How consistently have you been able to do that in the past?

2. How you define ego will directly determine how you can combat it correctly. How have you in the past, and how would you now, define ego?

3. Try to notice when you are ignoring the ego and when you try to fight against it?

Vanquish Ego

Lesson 5

To win, Sun Tzu says:

- Understand yourself, and not the enemy, and you suffer.
- Understand neither yourself nor the enemy, and you lose.
- Understand yourself and your enemy and you need not fear the result of a hundred battles

Vanquish Ego

You probably noticed a recurring theme in the above sayings – understanding. Let me tell you a story:

Years ago, when I was teaching 'A Course in Miracles' support groups in the New York City area wonderful, truly serious students attended. Two of them were a married couple. Each had his or her own copy of the 'Course' to study. Each of them, like so many students highlighted sentences and sometimes whole paragraphs in their personal copies that impacted them especially.

One evening at class I had occasion to notice their books sitting side by side on a table. With their permission I flipped through each book quickly noting with amusement what was highlighted. Easily almost half of each book was a bright yellow. Now, here's what amused me.

Vanquish Ego

The husband's 'Course' had yellow highlights on every uplifting poetically eloquent comment, prayer and explanation. The wife, on the other hand had highlighted every intense, sometimes dark and scary portrait of ego at work. Hmmm. If you read only the yellow in each book you would think there were actually two Course in Miracles.

There is a reason why both the radiant and the murky gloom are explained in sometimes redundantly spiraling passages throughout the 'Course'. We need to be able to recognize clearly the Voice for God as differentiated from the ego's Ninja Warriors. And it's not just to be able to distinguish between them. We also need time and training to learn to truly desire only the OneVoice that will bring us peace.

As Sun Tzu pointed out hundreds of years ago, recognizing and understanding the enemy a well as yourself is essential to success.

Vanquish Ego

Understand, recognize and choose correctly and we 'need not fear the result of a hundred battles.'

Some thoughts to contemplate...

1. If you haven't studied *'A Course in Miracles'* yet but could use a helpful overview of the dynamics of ego, try the previous mini course "Fast Track to Peace' or 'Hand in Hand'. You can find both in the left column of my blog either in paperback or e-book format.

2. Observe yourself and honestly notice if you are ignoring or denying emotions and responses that you are afraid to admit to.

3. Observe your interactions this week and notice how a greater understanding of the people around you and how your intimate interactions can change drastically with understanding and insight.

Vanquish Ego

Lesson 6

To win, Sun Tzu says:

Recognize when to engage

and when not to engage

Vanquish Ego

The battle ground is always within our minds. But instead we love to take the fight into the streets of our lives – finding fault with others, taking offense easily, loudly proclaiming our innocence at home, at work, at 'play'. So, before we tackle when to engage in battle and when not to engage let's remind ourselves where that battleground resides. In – Our - Mind. O.K. That being said loud and clear, let's move forward.

In lessons 4 and 5 we emphasized the importance of recognizing ego's Ninja Warriors in their camouflaged uniforms and understanding fully the weaponry they will use for attack. Now is a good time to spy on ego's headquarters and do deep recon of the enemy.

We learn that ego's plan is to protect us. Ego arrogantly believes it knows who we are and what

Vanquish Ego

we need to survive. Focused tightly on keeping our bodies alive and conquering all social encounters, ego creates its master strategies. Ego's logic: Keep our bodies alive and win in every social encounter, no matter the cost to our happiness, our comfort, our peace of mind or the effects on others.

Circled around ego are its three Ninja Warriors.

We notice the first Ninja Warrior slouching and complaining – its name is Guilt. Feelings of unworthiness, uselessness and despair flow over this warrior forming its weaponary that seep into our mind to debilitate us.

Trembling next to Guilt is the Ninja Warrior whose name is Fear. Cold fingers of panic are poking and thrusting from the Warrior reaching to back us into emotional corners.

Bold, loud, aggressive and ready to explode in a nano second at any perceived slight looms the final warrior whose name is Anger. This Ninja

Vanquish Ego

Warrior carries the heavy weapons of destruction. The first two warrior are inwardly focused to cause us the most personal pain, but Anger is always poised to attack and take the battle outside the mind, confusing us so we no longer know from where the true enemy threatens and where the battleground must be.

When must we engage these enemies? As soon as we catch a whiff of their presence. The clue? We will be unhappy, uncomfortable, irritable. And we must act quickly, as soon as we notice a lack of contentment. We must change our perspective, within our own mind.

When not to engage? When we believe the threat to our happiness and safety is attacking us from a cause outside of ourselves – the people around us, the government, the weather, the traffic patterns. And the list can go on and on.

Vanquish Ego

Exactly what to do when we must engage ego within the battleground of our minds? That will be another lesson.

Some thoughts to contemplate...

1. Notice how often you find the battleground outside you as people and events that disturb your contentment.

2. Review the three ego Ninja Warriors of guilt, fear, anger and make a point of labeling them by name each time your feel discomfort.

3. Make a commitment *to desire* the shifts in your own perspectives that can correct your feelings of guilt, fear or anger. This is a deceptively simple yet powerful step.

Vanquish Ego

Lesson 7

To win, Sun Tzu says:

Be vigilant and undeterred by old ways

Vanquish Ego

To paraphrase a quote from the movie 'The Godfather' and then immortalized in the T.V. show the 'Sopranos' – "Just when I think I'm out, they suck me back in!" And so, it goes with ego.

Here's a great quote from *'A Course in Miracles'* (*Text, Chapter 9, subheading 'The Two Evaluations'*) that speaks directly to this stealthy strategy of ego:

"The ego is deceived by everything you do, especially when you respond to the Holy Spirit, because at such time its confusion increases. The ego is, therefore, particularly likely to attack you when you react lovingly, because it has evaluated you as unloving and you are going against its judgment. The ego will attack your motives as soon as they become clearly out of accord with its perceptions of you. This is when it will shift abruptly from suspicion to viciousness. . ."

Vanquish Ego

Ever notice that exactly when you are at your highest, happiest, most content "Murphy's Law" falls like a cleaver slicing up your peace of mind? Paranoia, annoyance and outright fury rushes in to fill the vacuum now created in your mind. Ego has struck!

After all, we have spent a lifetime depending on ego's myopic perceptions of us and the world to 'keep us safe'. Wariness, unworthiness, anger and faultfinding, martyrdom and revenge have been our go-to strategies. But now, we are climbing way out on the new branch of trusting in the Holy Spirit, and away from all things 'ego'. Ego is not going to take this lying down.

Ego first makes us suspicious and questioning – we look back and notice how far away from the safety of ego's tree trunk we have climbed. Trust wavers, we feel the slippery fingers of ego's Ninja Warriors infiltrating our thinking and Bam! We scurry back to the familiar old ways

Vanquish Ego

of dealing with life. We worry, we attack, and we embrace being miserable once more.

Not to worry. We have come too far. We quickly notice how unpleasant the negative world of ego is. We once more choose peace, and as we look up, the hand of forgiveness is right in front of us, ready to lift us back into the bright new world of peace.

And you know what? We grab it!

Some thoughts to contemplate...

1. Remember the last time you felt particularly peaceful and then remember how quickly it took misery to suck away the pleasure.

2. Remind yourself throughout the day that you are practicing something that you don't fully trust yet and that you will usually slip back and forth between ego and the Holy Spirit

Vanquish Ego

fairly often. Just notice this, don't feel guilty. Just keep practicing.

3. Take time to meditate quietly each day visualizing the hand of peace reaching down for you, and you reaching and gasping it. Then rest in the comfort that brings.

Vanquish Ego

Lesson 8

To win, Sun Tzu says:

The supreme art of war is to subdue the enemy without fighting

Vanquish Ego

We must become the Peaceful Samurai. Our way will be different. Our way will lift us above the battleground with the wings of love and forgiveness. Our way will embrace not the ego's art of war, but instead the Holy Spirit's Art of Peace.

We begin with a quote *from 'A Course in Miracles"*, the Workbook, Lesson 153, "In my defenselessness my safety lies". Sounds counter-productive doesn't it? Maybe even paradoxical. So, let's walk through an everyday opportunity I just witnessed at the hair designer.

As my hair tech, the manager of the shop, was just finishing up with me she was asked to come to the front counter. There, I observed a gentleman clearly annoyed and loudly making his point. He had made an appointment for that specific time, and another lady was going to be

Vanquish Ego

worked on before him. The counter person as well as the manager assured him, he would be next in line and this would take only a few minutes. But, oh no, he repeatedly made his point that this was his allotted appointment time and it was wrong to wait. (Ego imperative: Always be in the right and anger is a great weapon!)

The manager kept insisting that it wouldn't be but a few minutes and after all (here comes ego's defenses - a nicely expressed dollop of guilt) when he goes to a doctor or dental office he rarely gets in at his appointed time.

The gentleman stood taller, pushed out his chest. (After all, accepting her logic would make him wrong and her right and humiliation just wasn't in his game plan.) He repeated his point, again and again, jabbing his finger on the counter, defending his position. The manager, feet spread leaning toward the man responded through gritted teeth her position. The battle lines were drawn.

Vanquish Ego

(Ego's Ninja Warriors were head to head, each battling to be more 'right' than the other.)

Thankfully a hair tech appeared and brought him back to her chair. I could hear his voice above the hum of hairdryers continuing to defend his position. The manager, finishing my hair, kept mumbling and defending her position. I was glad there was a hair dryer and no scissors in her hand.

Ego normalcy reigned. The ongoing everyday wars raged on. But, how can we be defenseless when someone is clearly making us wrong when we know we are right? Let's review.

- First stop as soon as the conflict starts.
- Now want something other than emotional tussles running your day.
- Then, here's a tricky one - Be willing to be wrong of your assessment of yourself and your opponent. This is hard because ego will want you to

Vanquish Ego

keep fighting to be 'right'. The fear of humiliation will be strong and your desire for peace will need to be stronger.

- Last, take a deep breath and risk asking humbly for help. Then wait for a miraculous and releasing new perspective of your encounter, trusting that this will release your guilt, your fears and your need to remain angry and combative.

Words and actions will naturally and gently fill your mind with a new forgiving view of your world. And as you share them not only you will be released, but your enemy will be released with you.

Peace can now be allowed to reign.

Vanquish Ego

Some thoughts to contemplate...

1. Observe your day and notice each time you feel the need to defend your position.

2. As often as necessary practice the four steps listed above in this lesson.

3. Review the full Lesson 153 from the *Workbook, 'A Course in Miracles.'*

Vanquish Ego

Lesson 9:

To win, Sun Tzu says:

He will win who takes the time to prepare

Vanquish Ego

So, you want to be a Peaceful Samurai. Cool. Go Peace! Go Samurais! Go...uh oh... "you mean I can't just put on my 'peace' cape and strut around being peaceful right off the bat? I actually have to train for a really long time to be one?" you ask. Yup.

Superheroes for peace take years, decades, even several lifetimes to create. And a good sense of what basic training is like is covered under the section *"What are the characteristics of a teacher of God,"* and Trust is listed as the first characteristic. (*'A Course in Miracles' Manual for Teachers*). The main point is that your training program will be the most challenging and rewarding rollercoaster ride you have ever taken. You will be placed into constant ego induced battles with ego's Ninja Warriors within your mind. Some you will overcome and many more you will flounder through and lose.

Vanquish Ego

Again, and again you will feel the exultation and release of accepting peace. And again, and again you will be tested and what you desire most will seemingly be taken from you. Becoming disappointed, depressed, disenchanted and down right bedeveiled will occur more often than not. But, take heart. Standing with you every step of the way are Mighty Companions, the Peaceful Samurais that have gone before.

Trust is explained as the first and perhaps most pivotal characteristic of the advanced teacher of God, or what we are calling the Peaceful Samurai. You will find a very special and important word in that sentence – advanced – the officers. You become a teacher of God or a bottom of the heap private in the army of Peaceful Samurais as soon as you choose to set aside ego, if only for a moment, and choose the forgiving answer instead. But, to become an advanced teacher of God, an officer, a true super hero

Vanquish Ego

Peaceful Samurai you will need to choose forgiveness again, and again, and again and . . . (you get the idea).

This is why you are here, and this is your calling. The world is in need of healing and you have been chosen to enlist. You are reading this mini course, so you already have your helmet and shield and willingness.

Now, get on with your training. Ego's Ninja Warriors are gathering and preparing for battle.

Some thoughts to contemplate...

1. How many years does it take to become a doctor? To become a specialist in a field? To become world renowned as the best? Now, compare that to your spiritual studies and the time you have given them.

2. Over your lifetime thus far, as well as the time you may have been studying

Vanquish Ego

spirituality, how often have you already had to face disaster and loss? How well did you handle it?

3. Take time each day to quietly sit with the Mighty Companions that surround you and rest in their strength.

Vanquish Ego

Lesson 10

To win, Sun Tzu says:

Build your opponent a golden bridge to retreat across

Vanquish Ego

What a lovely vision. As flutes and harps play a radiant bridge leads our enemies over and away to safety... WAIT! Stop the music! Hold the horses! You mean we are supposed to let these nasty Ninja Warriors get away? Aren't we supposed to smash them to dust? Smite them with righteousness? Give these suckers a good thrashing, and then some?!

That does sound a little satisfying, but look again, this is ego's tactic – crush the enemy, the more pain the better. However, there IS a better way.

Up to now most of our lessons have covered some (certainly not all) of the important issues covered in *'A Course in Miracles' Textbook*. The Text helps us learn to recognize the ego in all its sneaky 'glory' and understand its strategies with their painful and unhappy effects on us. All thirty-one chapters take us on a spiraling and deepening

Vanquish Ego

journey into the discovery of ego, as well as the Holy Spirit and the peaceful Answer offered. We learn why choosing peace is a really, really good idea.

How to choose peace is then the task of the Workbook, your basic training as a Peaceful Samurai. When completed after 365 lessons, and at least a full year, we will have created the habits that, when practiced consistently, last a lifetime. We learn to build a golden bridge. Let's see what that means.

Ego battles, the Holy Spirit suggests we fly above the battle ground, observe our thoughts that give rise to ego and pain and just Let Them Go.

Like clouds drifting across our minds, we can watch them and release them. Here they cross the golden bridge of forgiveness transformed into simple mist that simply floats away.

Each time we allow the Holy Spirit to change our view of the guilts, the fears, the angers

Vanquish Ego

that fill our minds, to opportunities of renewal and love, we add another gold bar to the bridge that ego and its Ninja Warriors can gently disappear across.

We do need to be willing to allow this to happen.

We do need to be willing to see our highly cherished judgments differently.

We do need to want contentment rather than the addictive emotions of unworthiness, worry and aggression.

This mini-course can only introduce you to these concepts or give your on-going studies and practices an extra turbo-charge. For real change I recommend doing and then consistently practicing the lessons from the Workbook.

Vanquish Ego

Some thoughts to contemplate...

1. *An important review of the characteristics of the Peaceful Samurai will be a last contemplation for this mini course:*
   *'A Course in Miracles' Manual for Teachers states, "...in time it can be said that the **advanced** teachers of God have the following characteristics: .."*

Study all of these characteristics and practice them every day. Use them as your helmet, your shield, your strategies for victory.

Then be assured - you will rise above ego's battleground triumphant as the Peaceful Samurai.

Vanquish Ego

Trust

1. Contemplate why all the following characteristics of the Peaceful Samurai will rest on Trust.

Honesty

2. Honesty rests on consistency and therefore removes deceit. Observe how consistent you are in all that you do and say.

Tolerance

3. Tolerance occurs when there is no judgment. Test yourself and see how you judge in the smallest ways and vow to do better.

Vanquish Ego

Gentleness

4.　Do no harm. These leads directly to gentleness. And emotional harm occurs when we make anyone, ourselves included, feel guilty. Make great effort in extending a sense of innocence and forgiveness to all.

Joy

5. The opposite of suffering is joyfulness. 'A Course in Miracles' states 'to heal is to make joyful.' Make lightheartedness your goal.

Defenselessness

6. When you realize ego's limited view of the world leads directly to feeling alone and unworthy, then you can choose to focus on the reality of oneness and peace. Notice how

this removes fear and the need to set up defenses.

Generosity

7. To give away love and joy cannot result in loss. You can't give love unless you are feeling loving. You can't give joy unless you are laughing also. These are the only important treasures and they can never be lost. Enjoy giving these gifts as much as possible!

Patience

8. Each day can now be released into holy instants where time becomes less and less important. Meditate and find this timeless space and take it into your days.

Faithfulness

9. Accept that Something within you, and within everyone else, is in charge in ALL

Vanquish Ego

MATTERS. Not in only some problems, not some challenges, not some worries, but the Answer is there for every big and every itty bitty issue. This will take great discipline, as will all the other characteristics that come before. It's time to just 'do it!'

Open-mindedness

10. Acceptance means lack of judgement. The natural expression is forgiveness. You recognize that what has been done is a mistake and seeing innocence in others, as well as yourself brings total release. Become the Peaceful Samurai by turning all thoughts, all judgments, and unhappy feelings over to the Inner Voice for correction.

Vanquish Ego

Now, walk through this world with only the weapon of Loving Forgiveness and become a hero for the world.

Made in the USA
Las Vegas, NV
16 June 2022